Mandala Designs
Coloring Book Volume 1

INTRODUCTION

According to the Encyclopedia Britannica mandala (MUHN-da-la) is defined as "a diagram seen in place of the universe that is utilized in sacred rites and also as a meditation instrument. The mandala works as a point of collection for universal forces. 'Entering' the mandala mentally and gearing toward its center, one is protected via the cosmic methods of disintegration and reintegration. "Essentially, mandala is freely interpreted from old Indian Sanskrit to mean circle. These specific circles are dominant symbols that several cultures have used for several thousands of years to symbolize balance, the circle of life, and a sense of unity linking with everything. Buddhists have been helping them free their minds stay focused, create room for meditation over the centuries with mandala. With you having the Mandala Coloring Book, you are open to the same possibilities.

Luckily, for you to enjoy all the benefits enjoyed by the Buddhists, you are not necessarily going to stare at the mandala in attempt to empty your mind. You will get all the guide you need to get into the mandala and taste from most of the real physical and therapeutic benefits by simply coloring in the 100 mandalas discovered throughout this book, as well as: translate

- Relaxation
- A sense of well-being
- Increased focus
- Increased creativity
- Reduced blood pressure
- Reduced stress and anxiety

Does this work, and how? The act of coloring drives your mind to center on the current task, filling in the mandala that doesn't allow for it to focus on stress, fear, and worry. Reducing or controlling these negative thoughts develops a sense of balance which has the backings of the inherent Meditative worth of the mandala. You will discover that you now live a much happier and healthier life that is connected with your surrounding after taking out little time coloring and allowing your meditative mind wonder. You are not far from having a clear mind and a healthy body through meditation, so why not grab that pencil and free up your mind.

HOW TO USE THIS BOOK

Startup meditation routine by selecting the materials you would need for your coloring. What to use differs from choice. There are people who are comfortable using pencils, crayons, felt tip pens, or even paints. When marking out your preference, consider if you would prefer your color to be blended and shaded (as you do with your pencils) or if the bright solid colors that you make out with paints and felt-tip pens. Whatever your choice, it is just perfect; the most important is for you to choose the one that you are happy with.

The next thing to do is, go over the book and you will get to a mandala page that would speak to you. Stop at that page; your inner mind will tell you what it requires and whatever mandala you choose at that moment will be your right meditative tool. Be aware that some mandalas have the ability to receive color faster than others. Be conscious of time because you don't have much time available. Would you prefer to complete every coloring less than one session? Or are you comfortable with finishing up over time?

Immediately your materials are all set with your mandala selected, you are good to go with coloring. The question is how I am to start? Selecting your colors is a highly personal thing, you shouldn't need a 2nd party to tell you the colors that you should or shouldn't apply on any mandala. There is nothing wrong for you to lay out your colored pencils or crayon before you and select at random if that is what you want. You will color your mandala the way it should be. If you prefer, you can use your mood or choice to decide on the colors you will use, that is also okay. Do not forget that different colors stand for different things. For instance:

- *White = purity, innocence, positivity*
- *Red = passion, strength, power, danger*
- *Orange = enthusiasm, happiness, creativity*
- *Yellow = energy, intelligence, joy*
- *Green = growth, harmony, fertility*
- *Blue = loyalty, wisdom, truth*
- *Violet = nobility, wealth, ambition*
- *Black = evil, death, mystery*

Well, there is no doubt that color is just a color sometimes, but having the colors symbol in mind before choosing can facilitate a quicker access to your subconscious mind.

No matter where you start your mandala coloring from, either from the inside or outside you will also get insight to you meditation and mind. People have been of the opinion that when you start coloring the mandala from the edge (outside) and then take an inward step to the center, this exploration can enhance your connectivity to the world around you. Also, it is a familiar trend to have the mandala colored in a symmetrical fashion that represents balance and order. This can either be via complex radial symmetry or straightforward mirror symmetry, working outward from the center in radial-type fashion.

There is no doubt that you will find each mandala unique in its color and design, so relax with a deep breath, set aside all your worries and let the coloring begin.

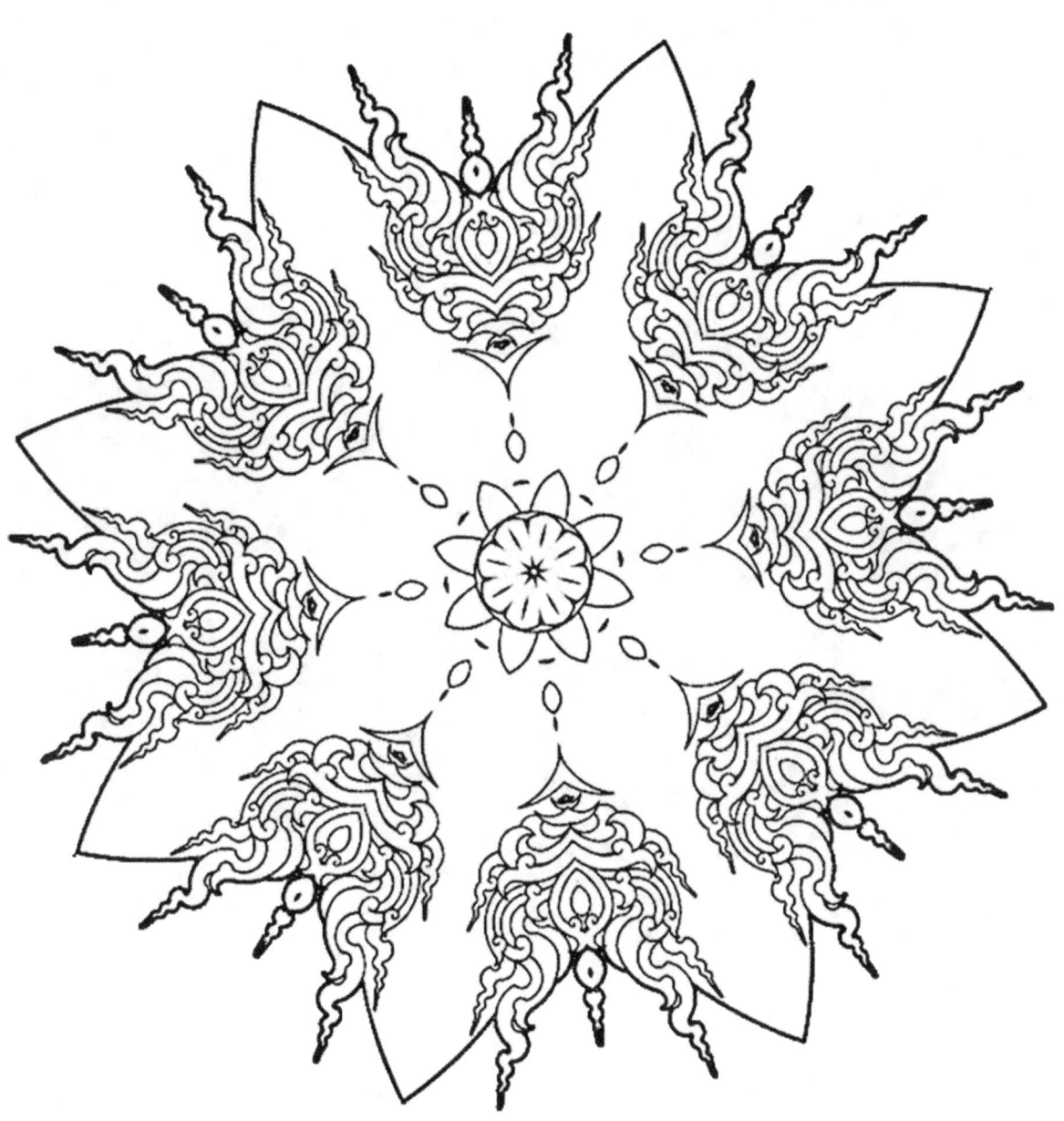

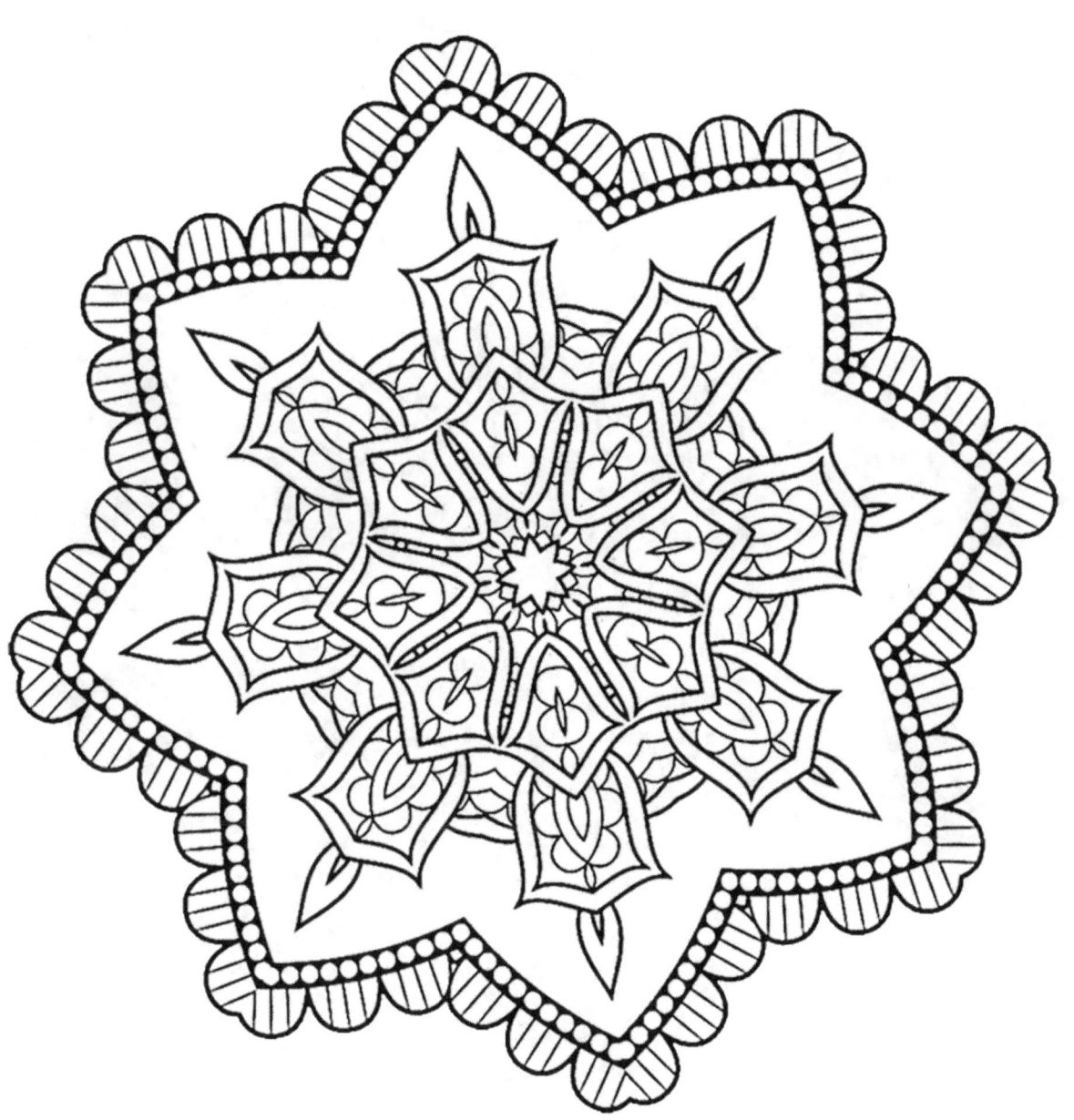

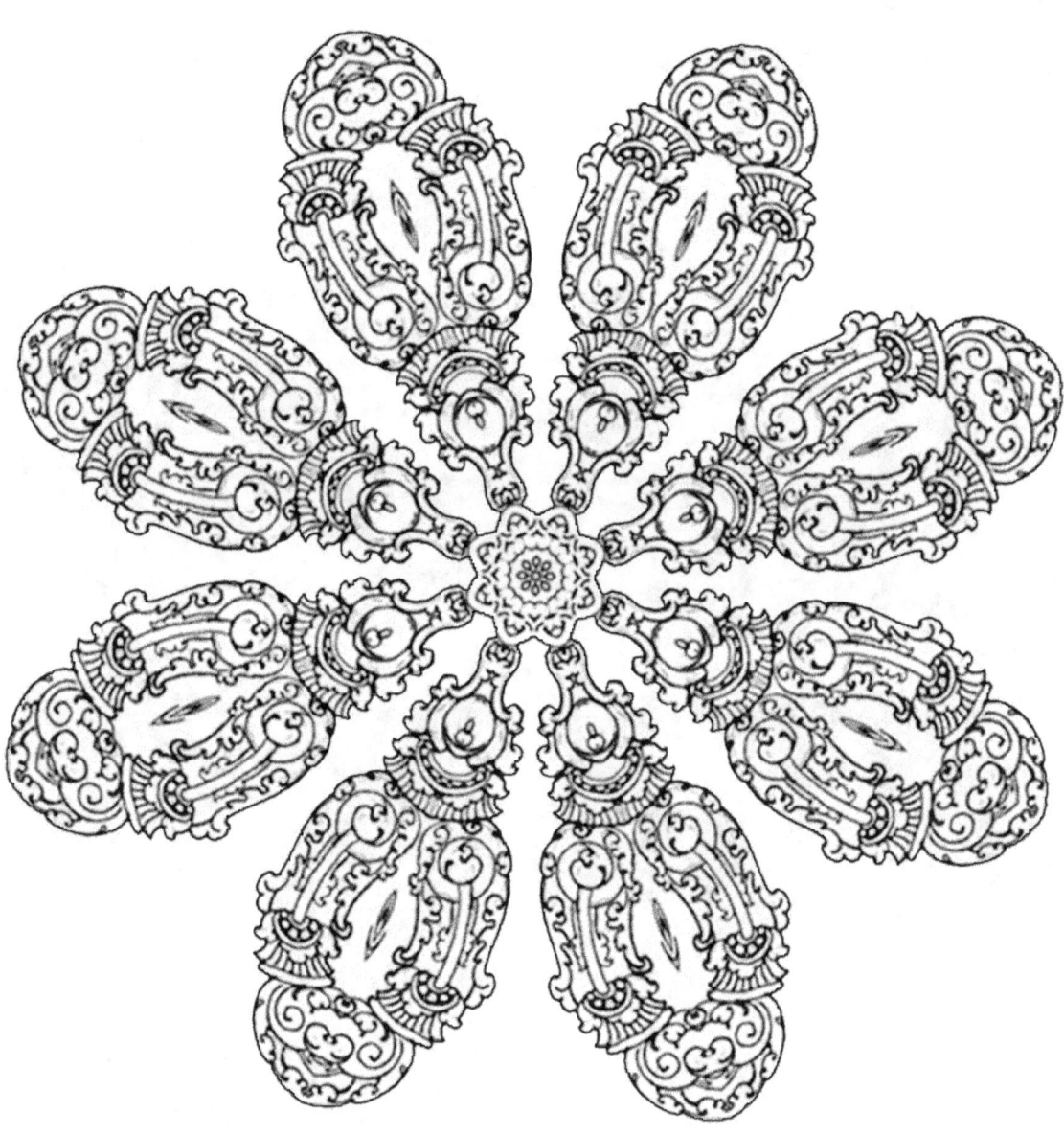

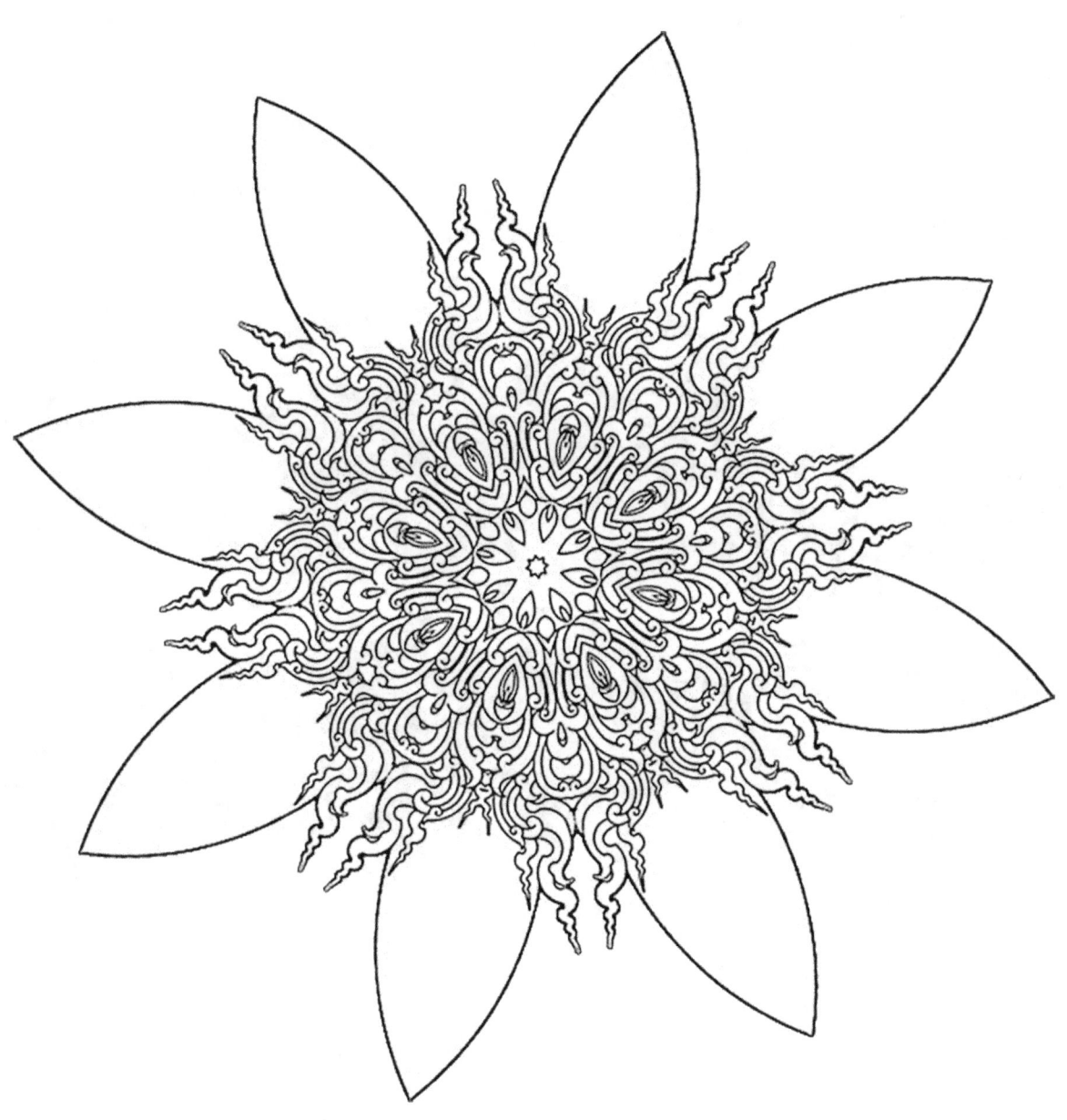

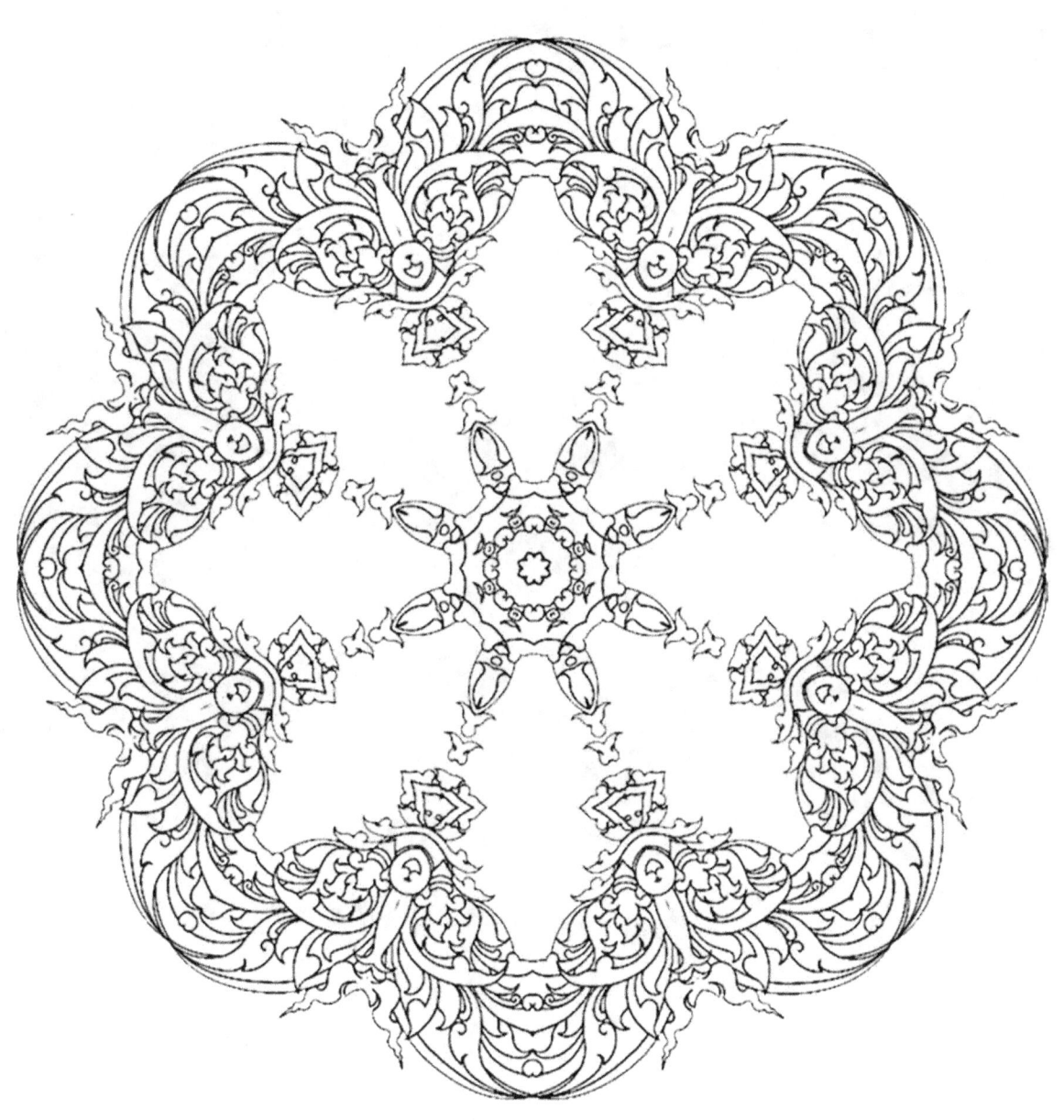

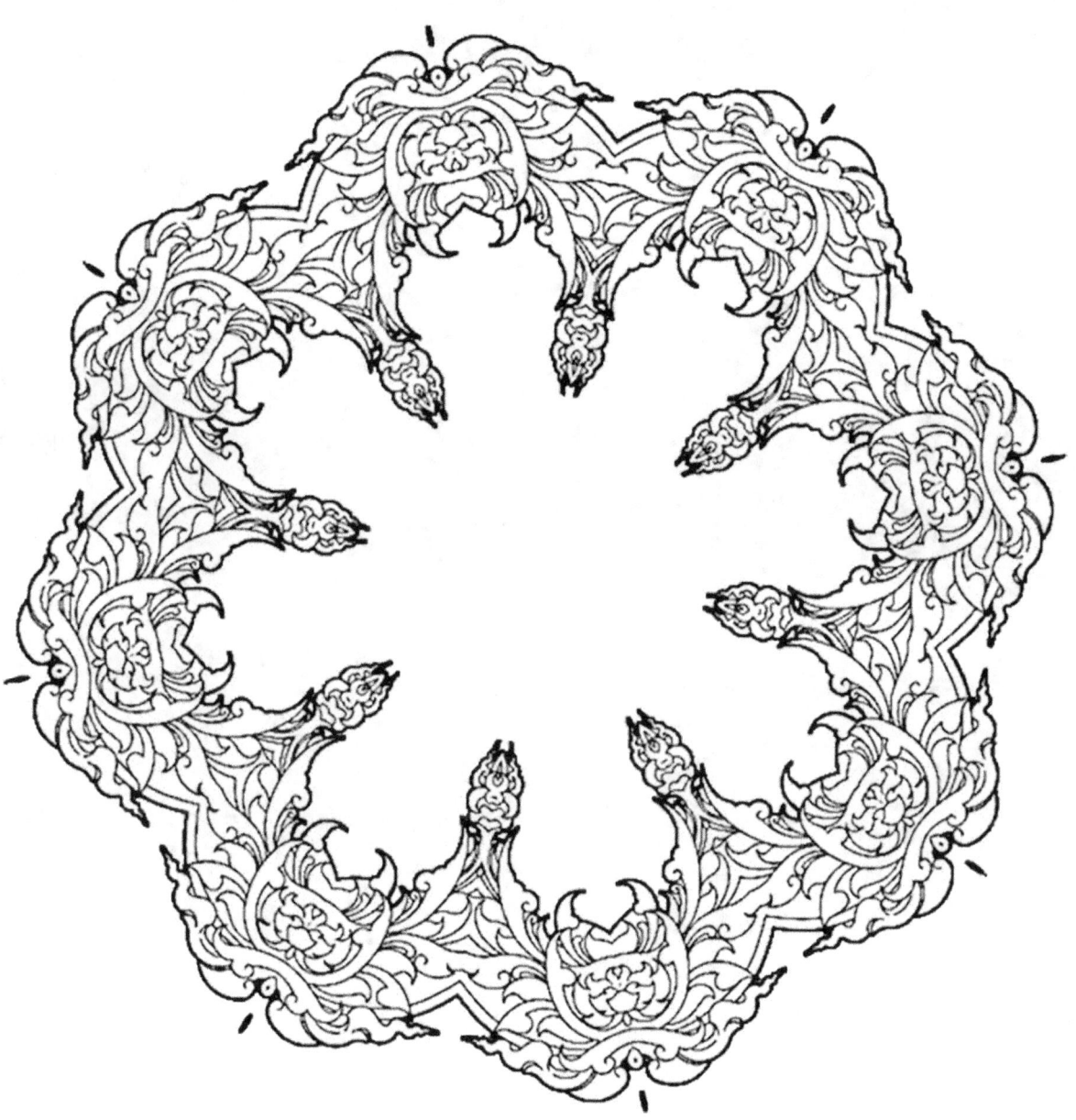

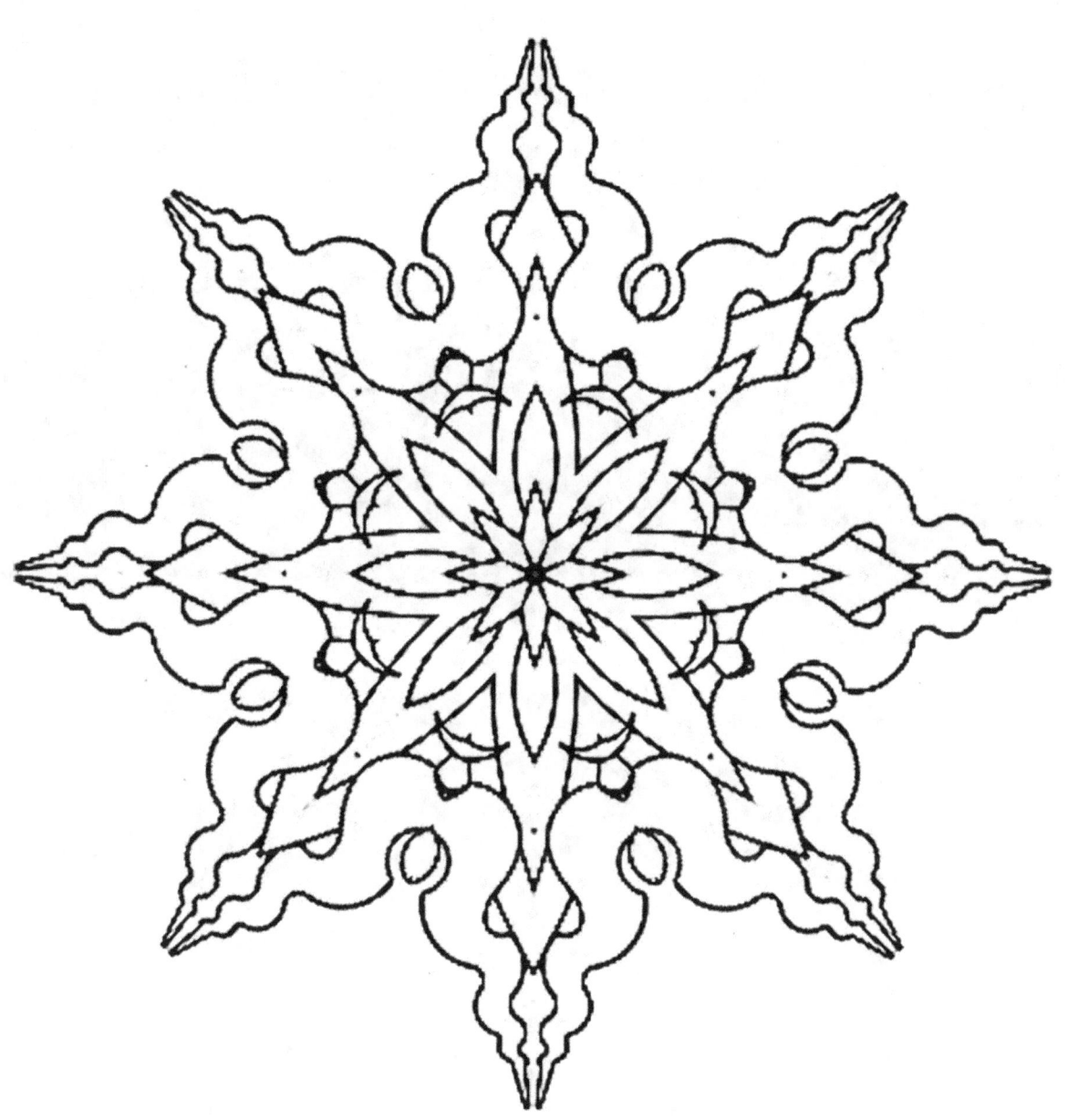

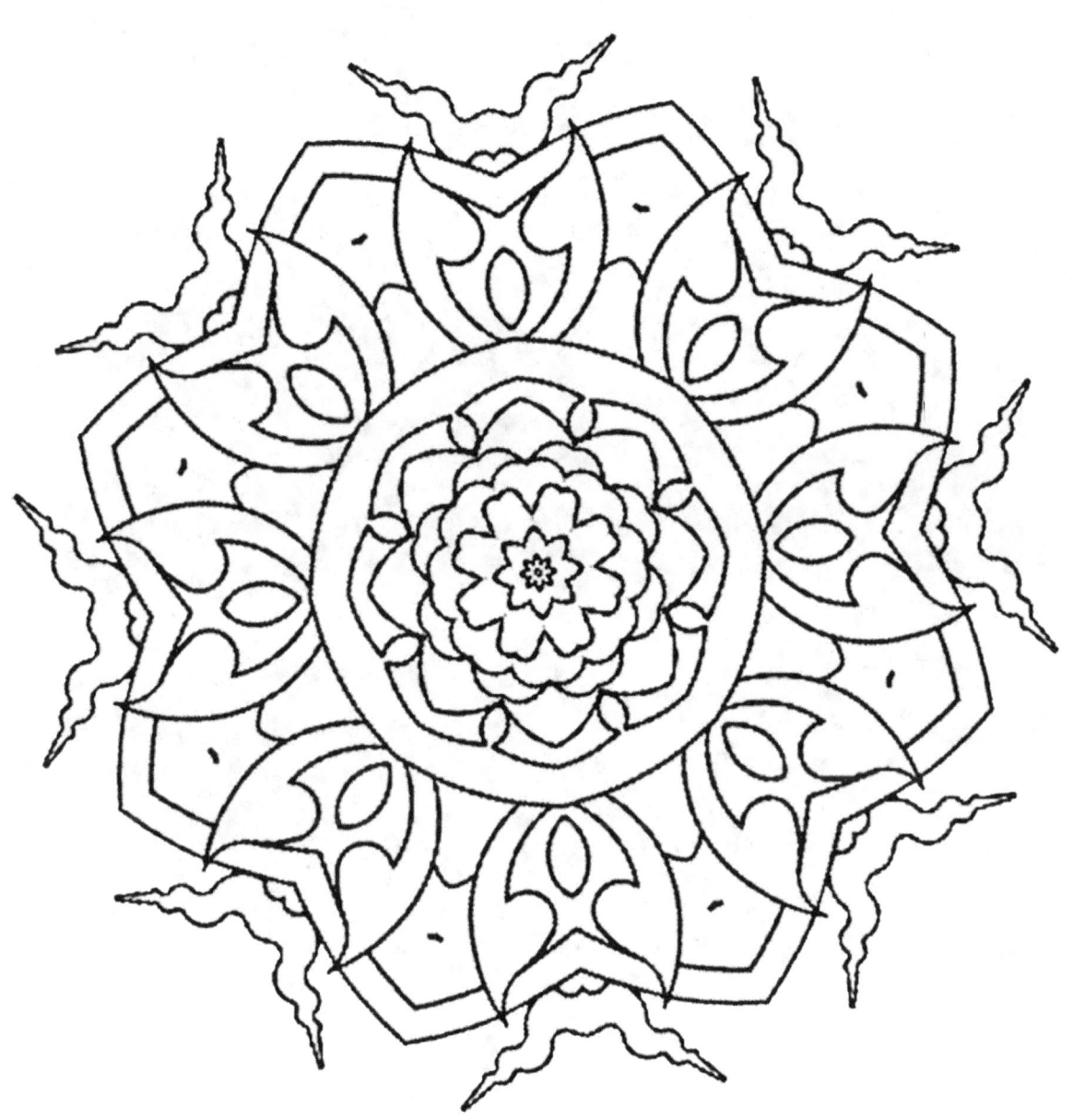

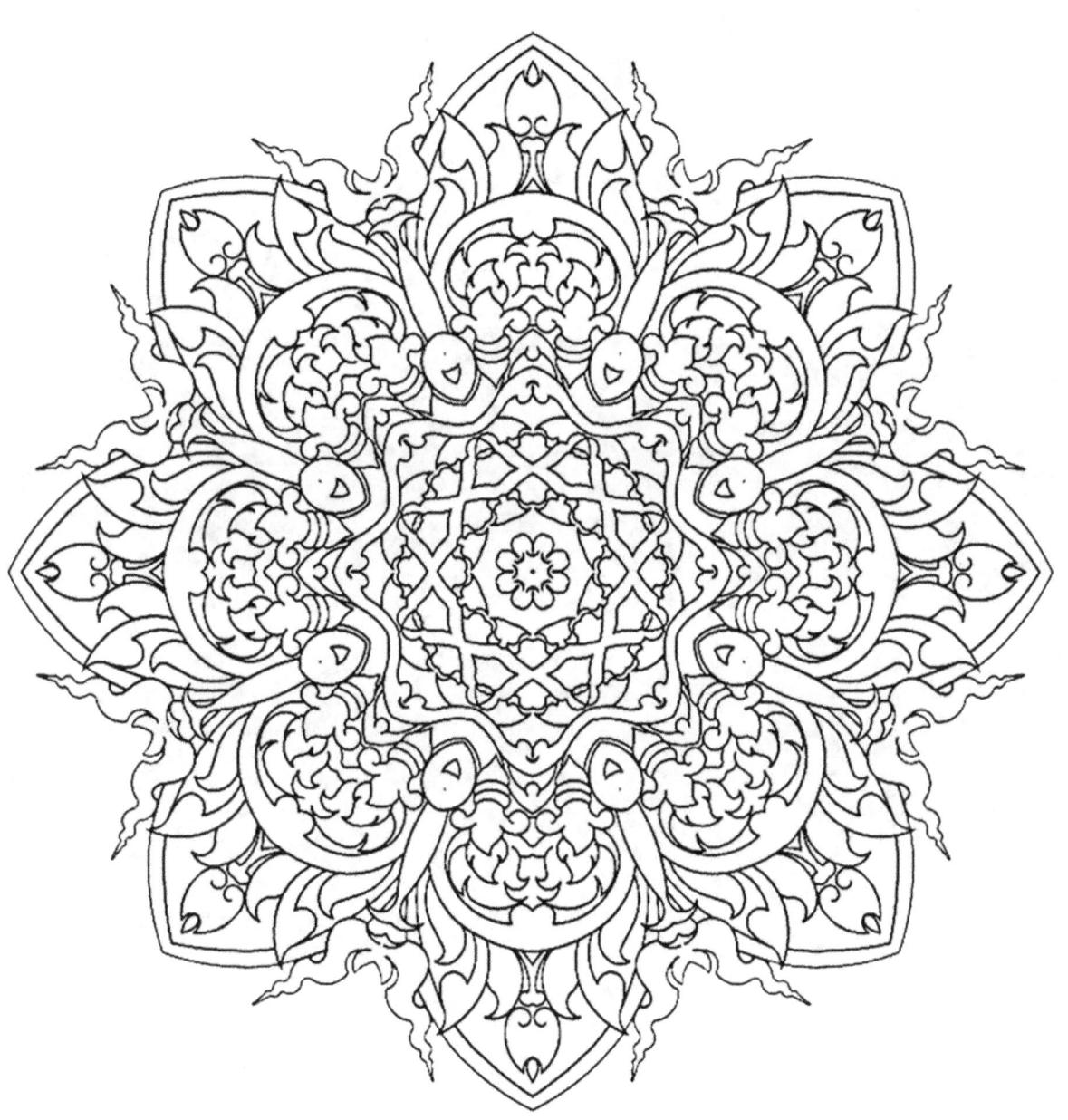

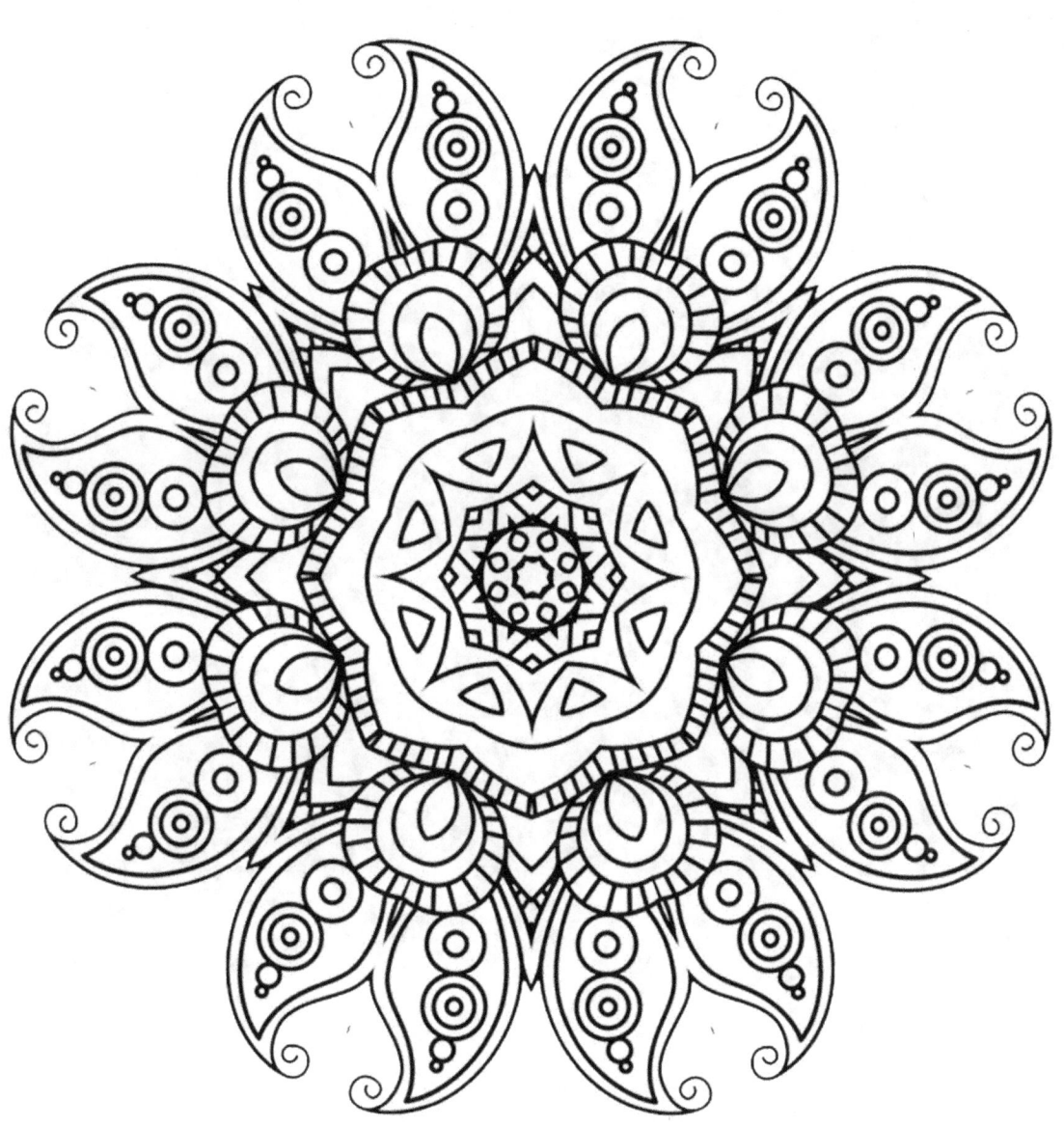

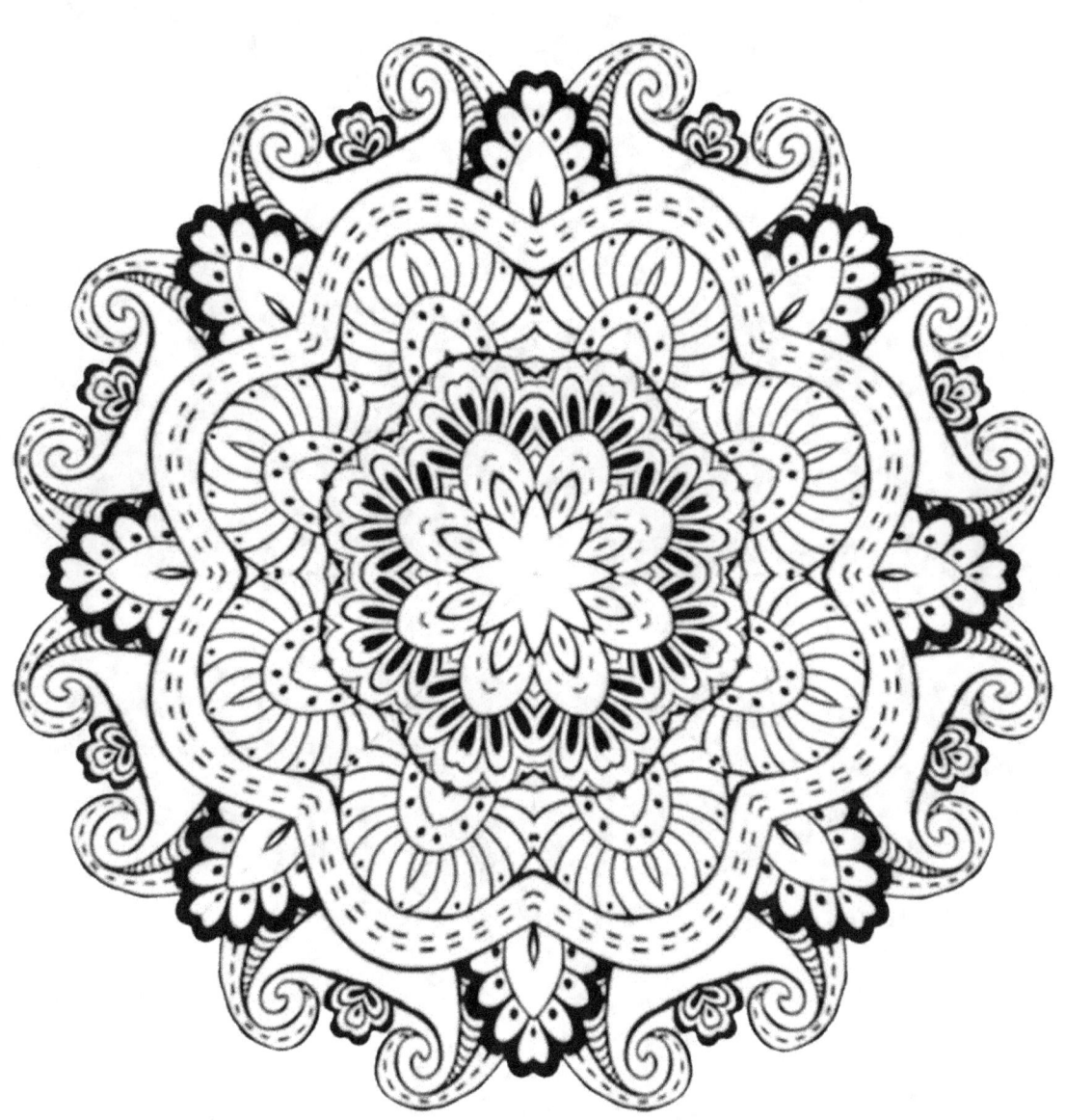

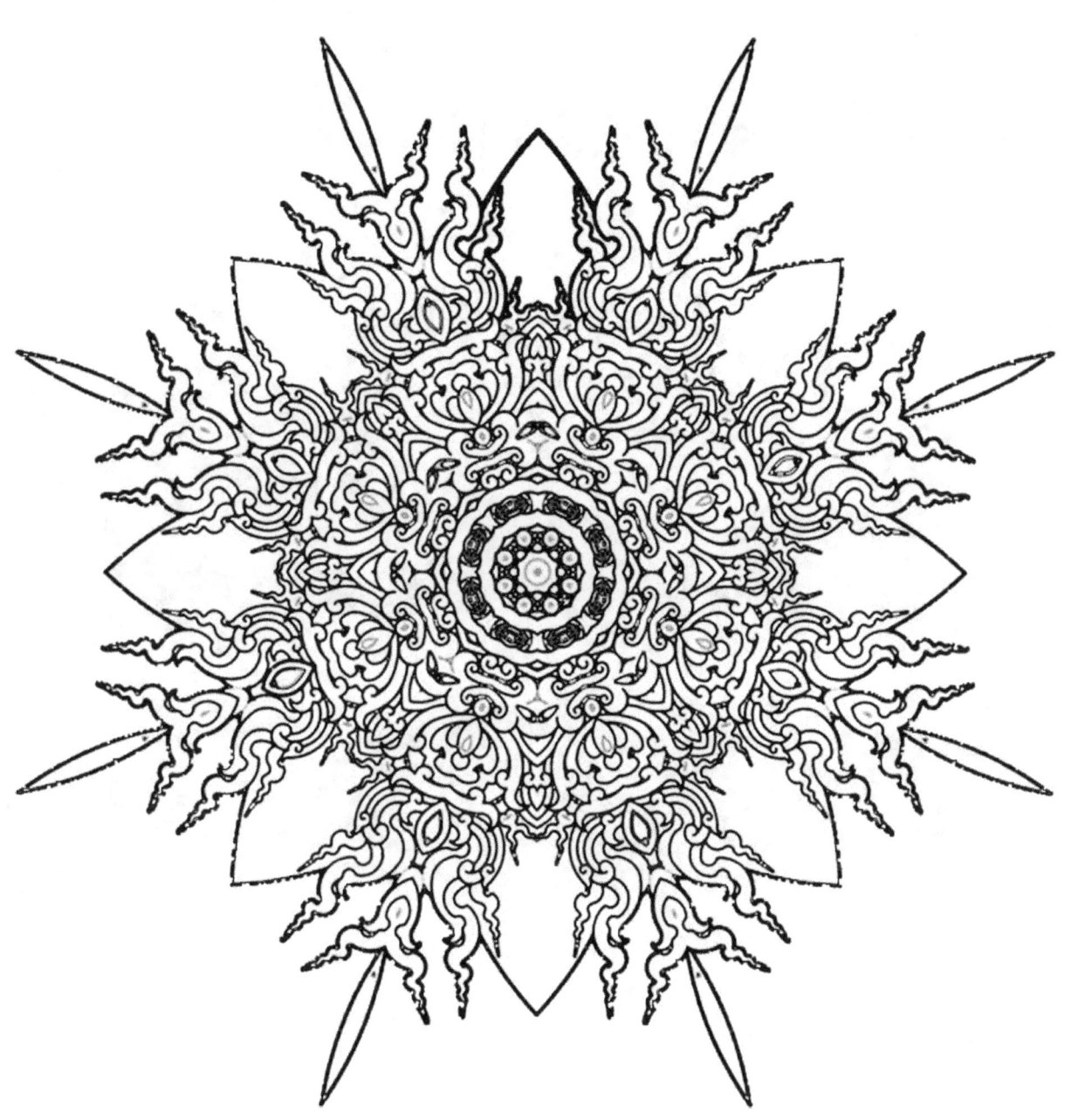

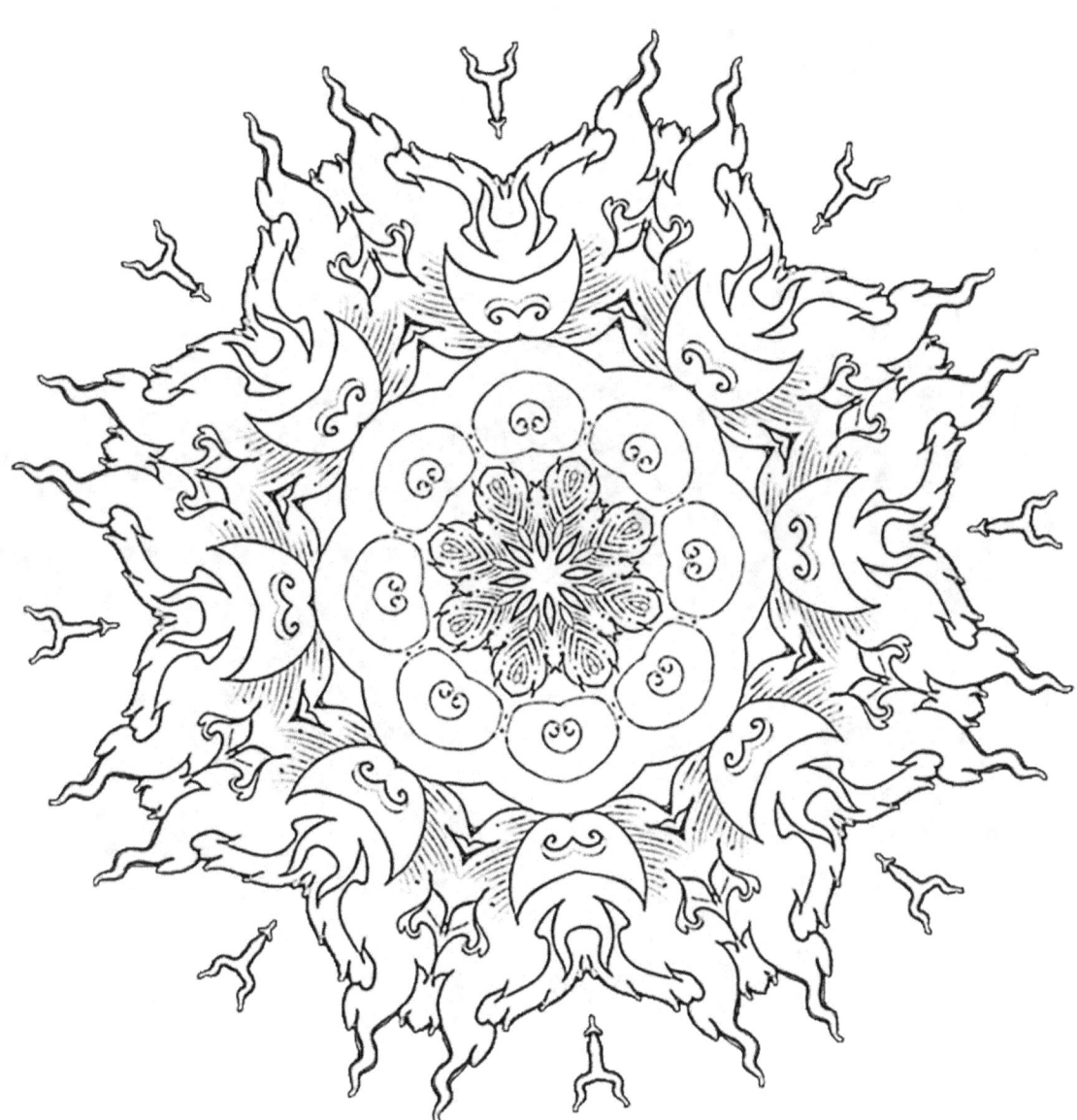

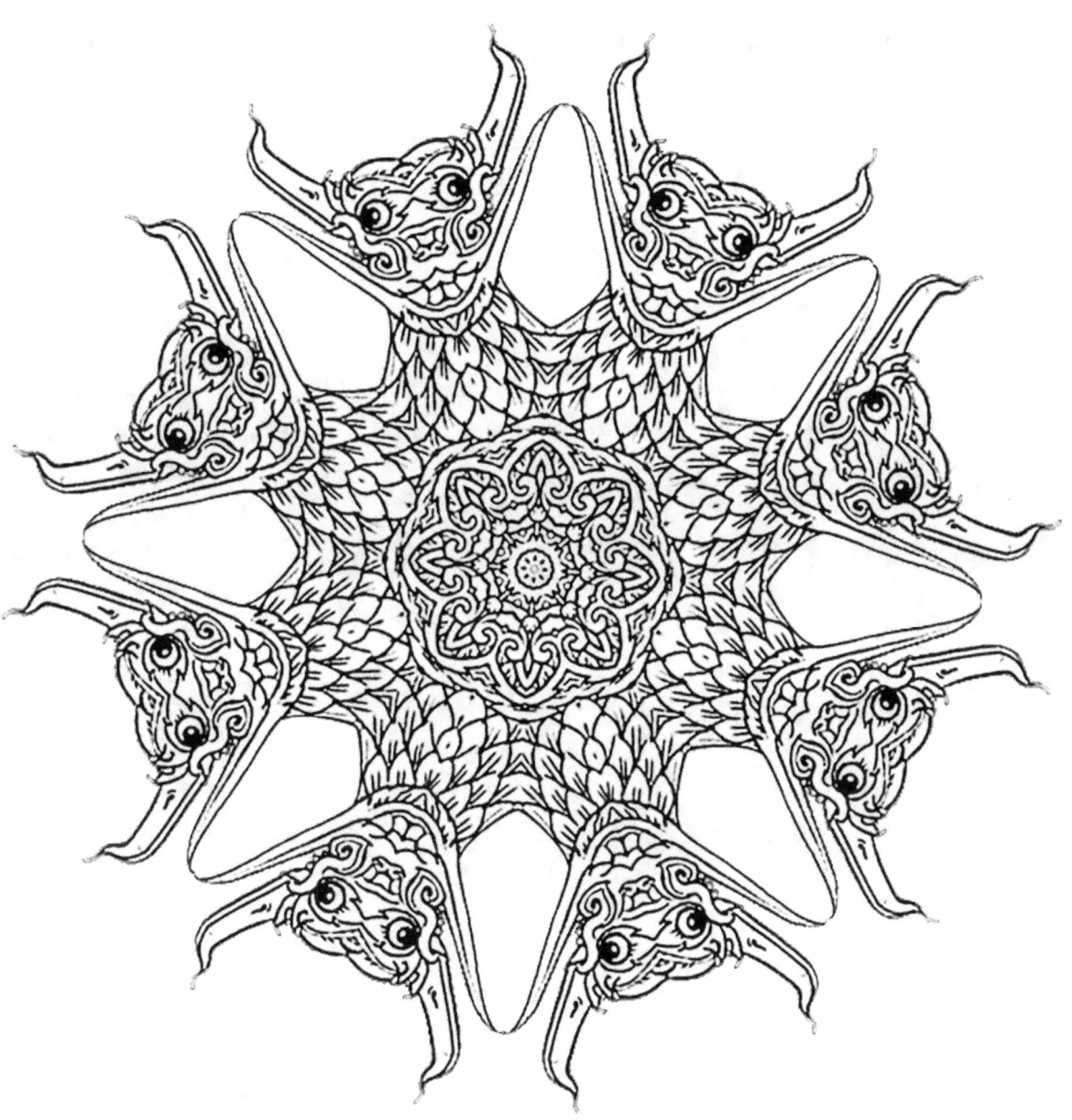

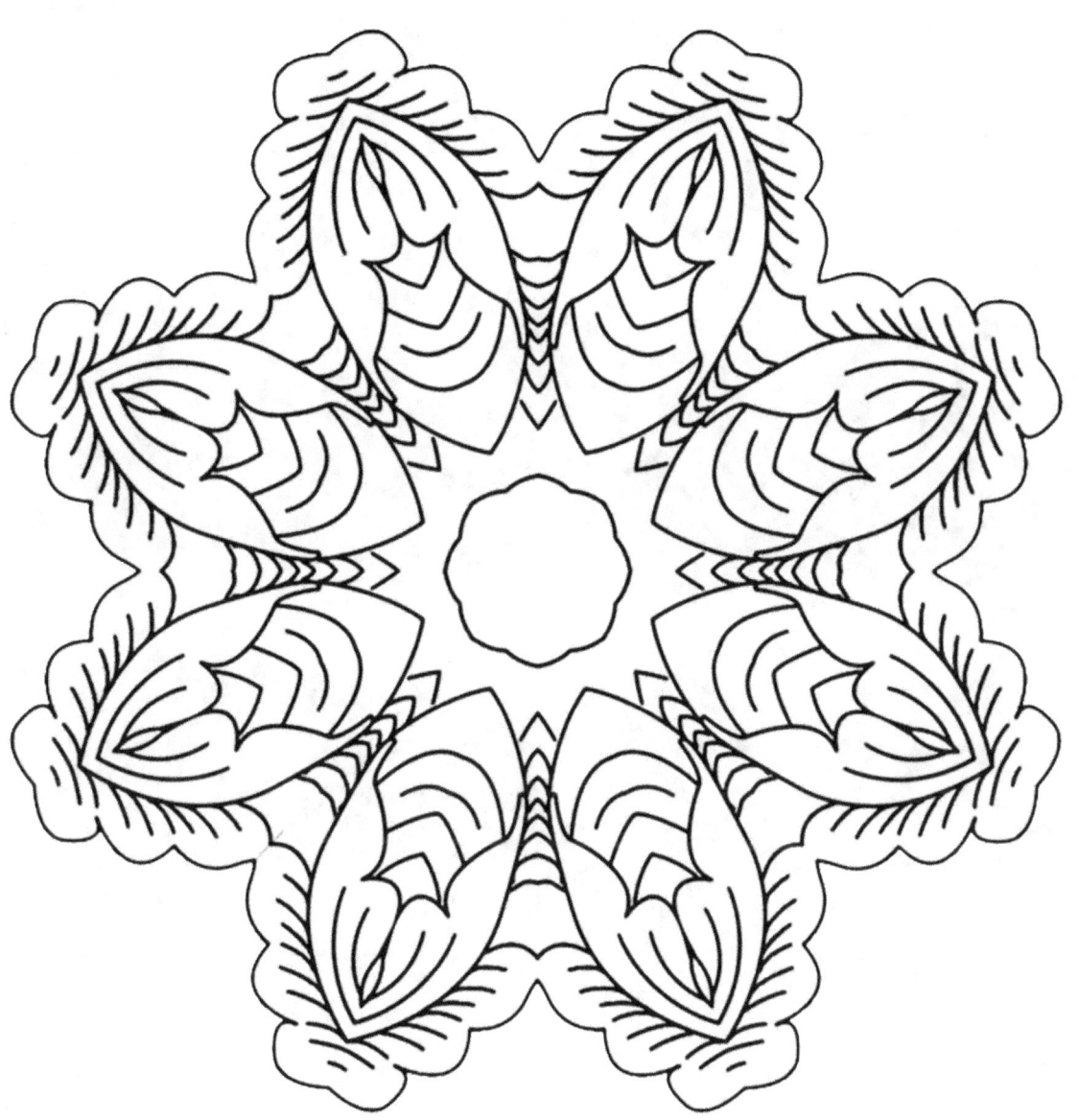

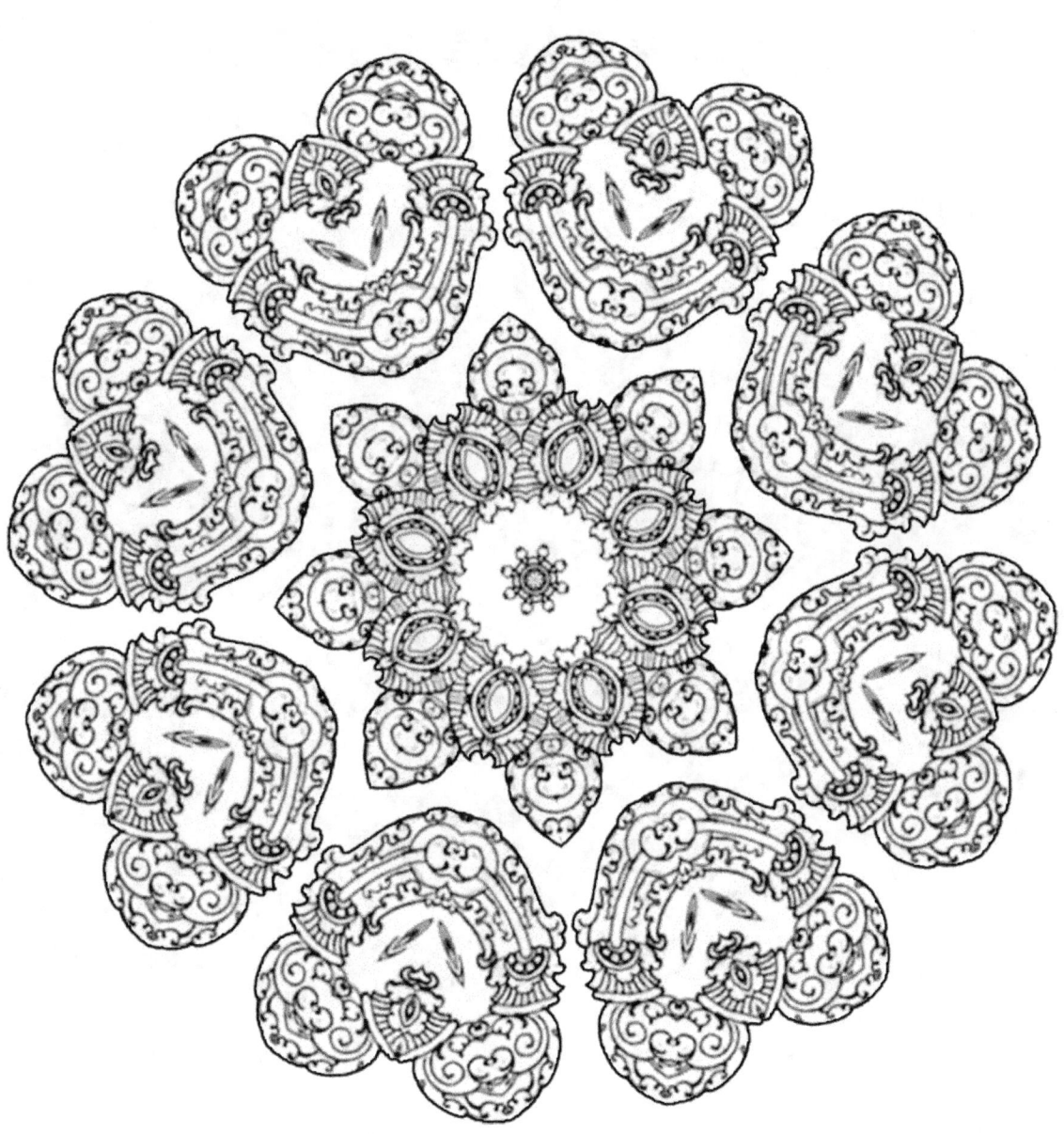

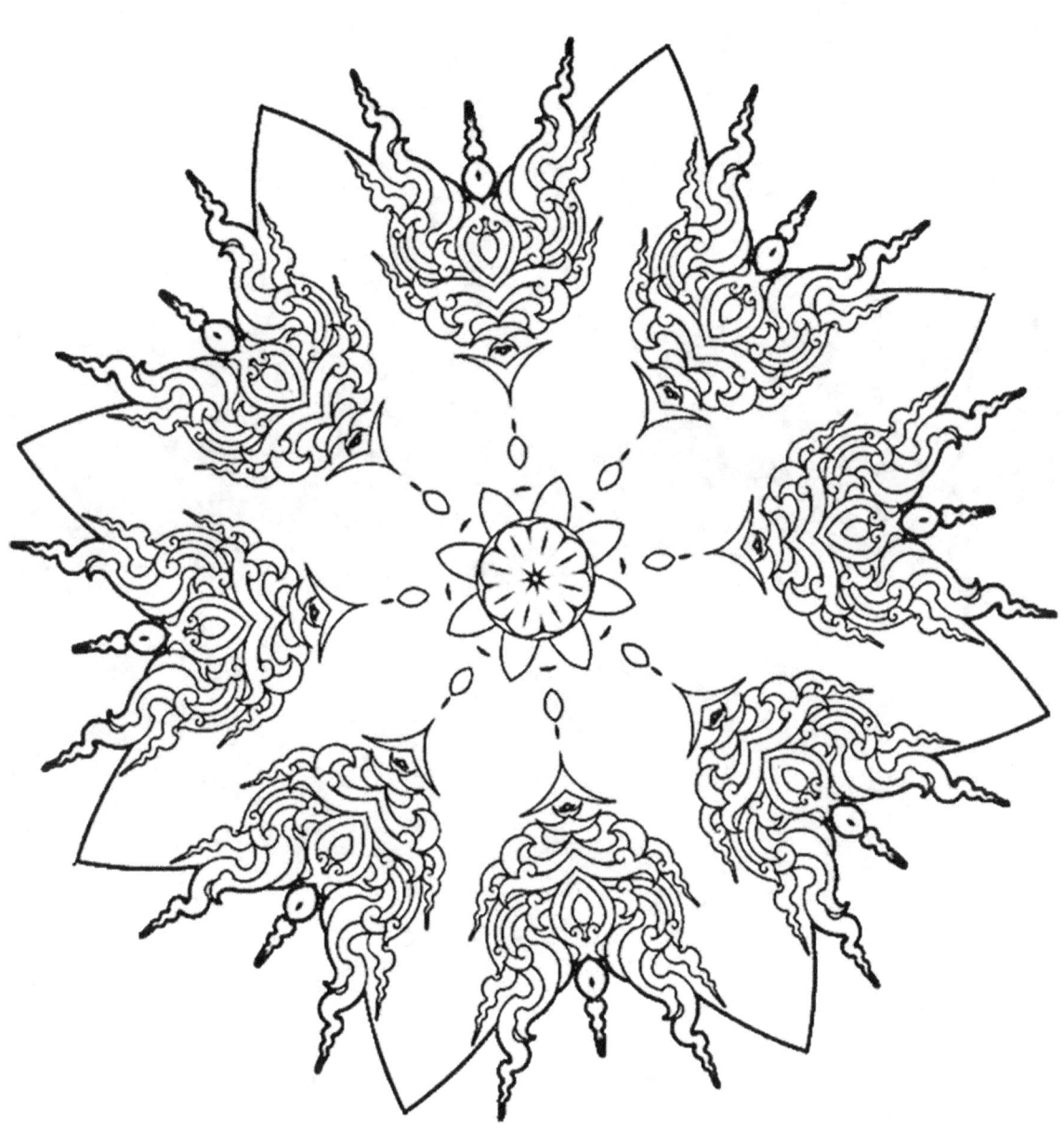

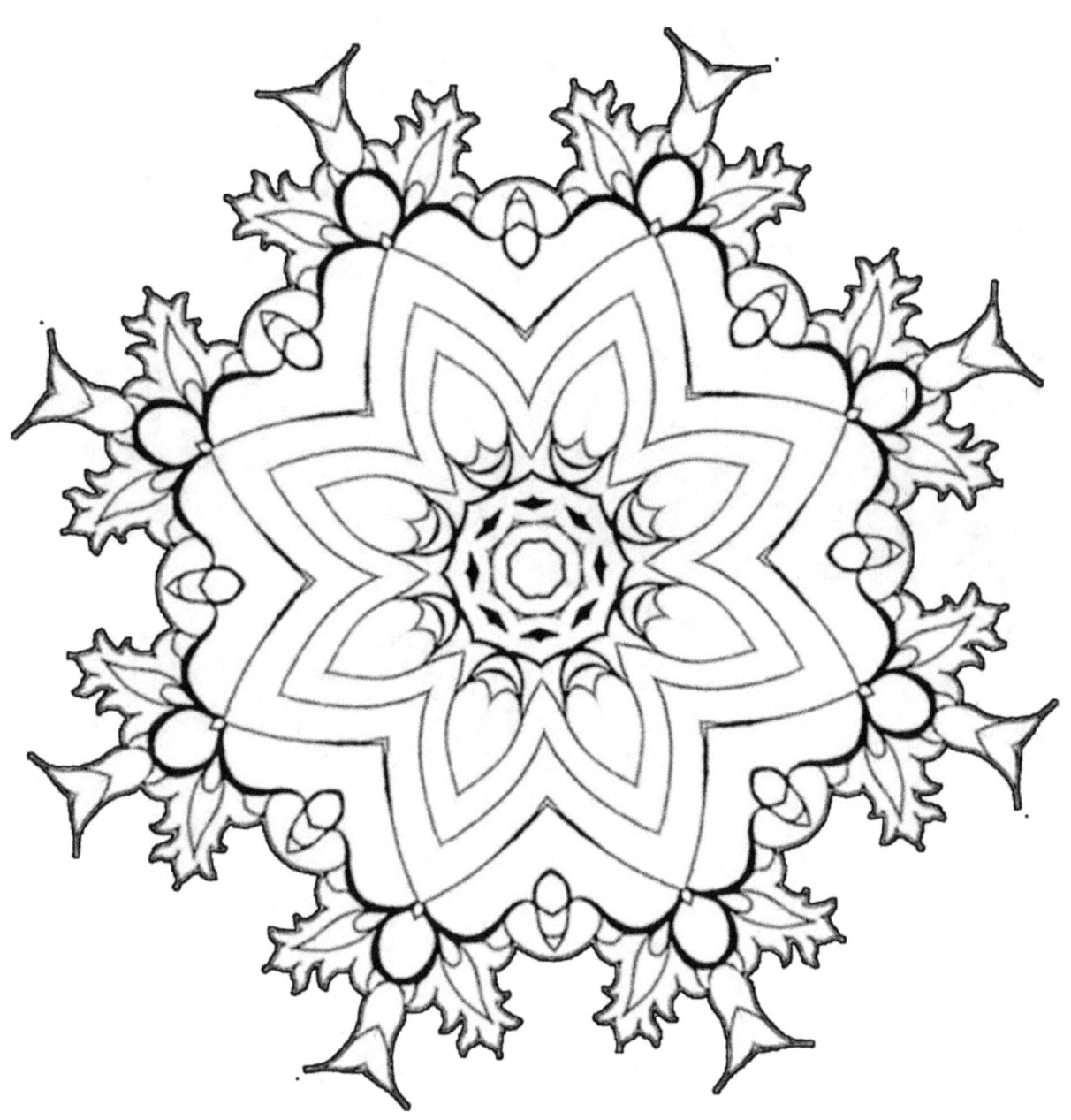

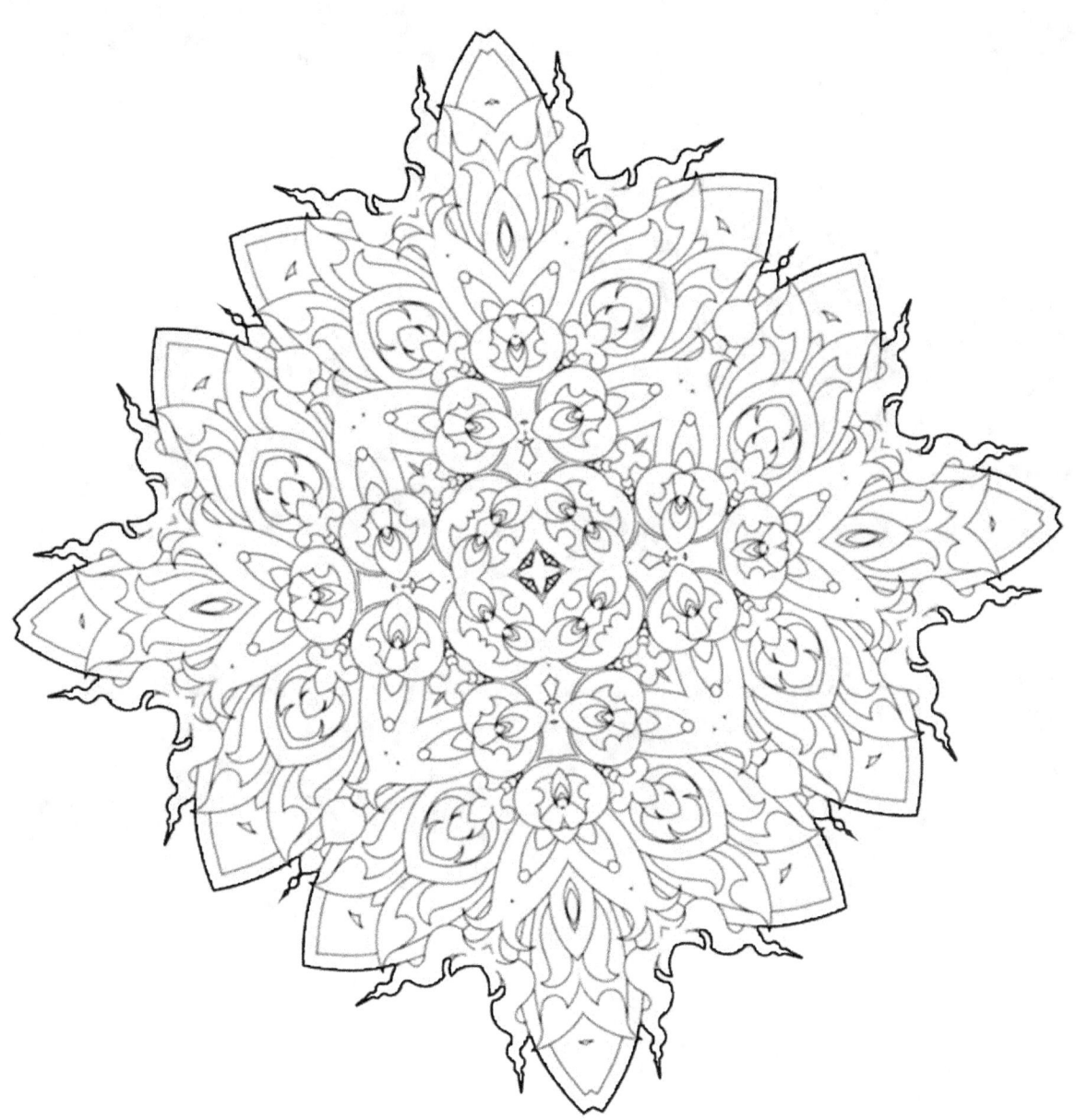

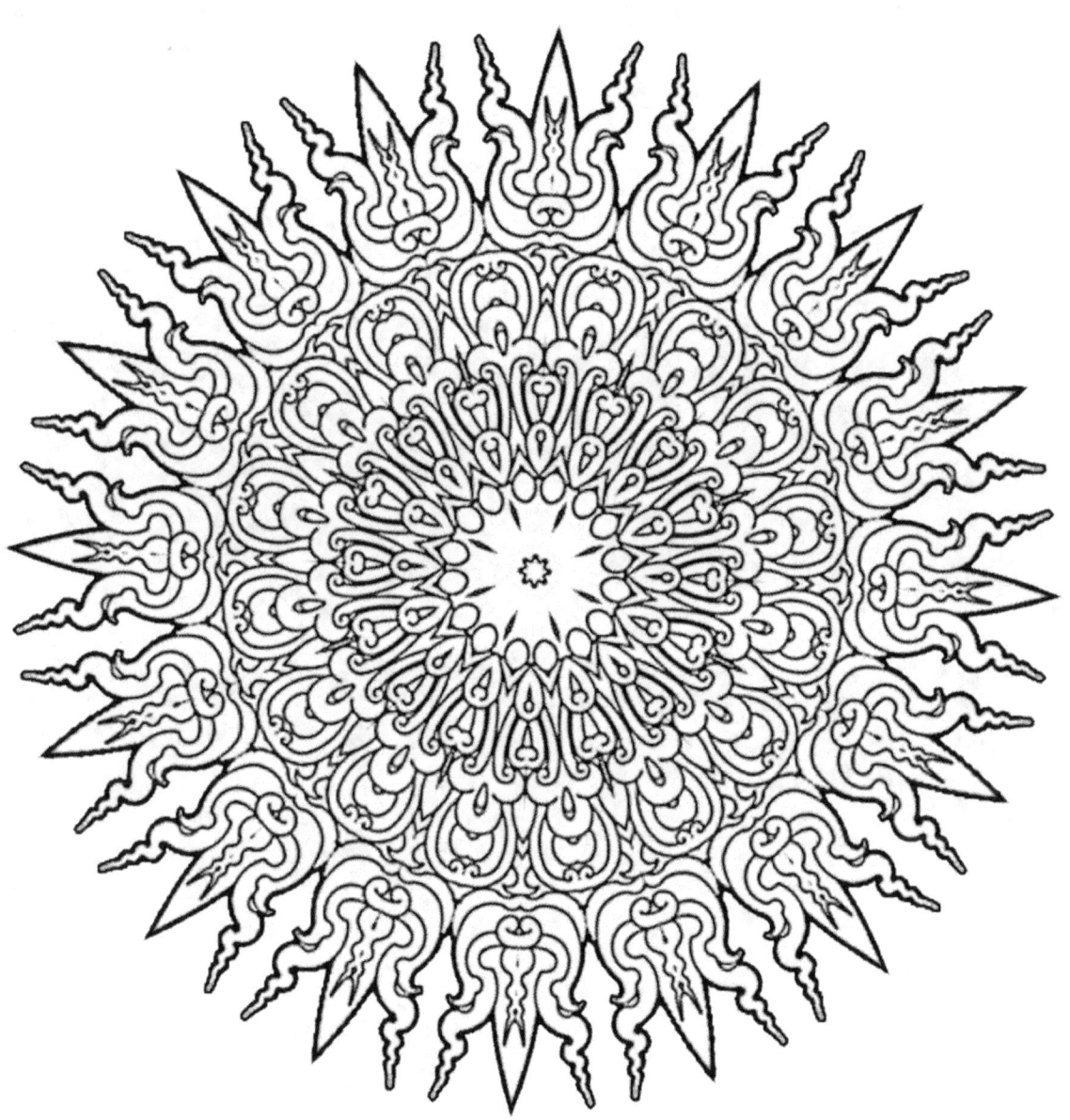

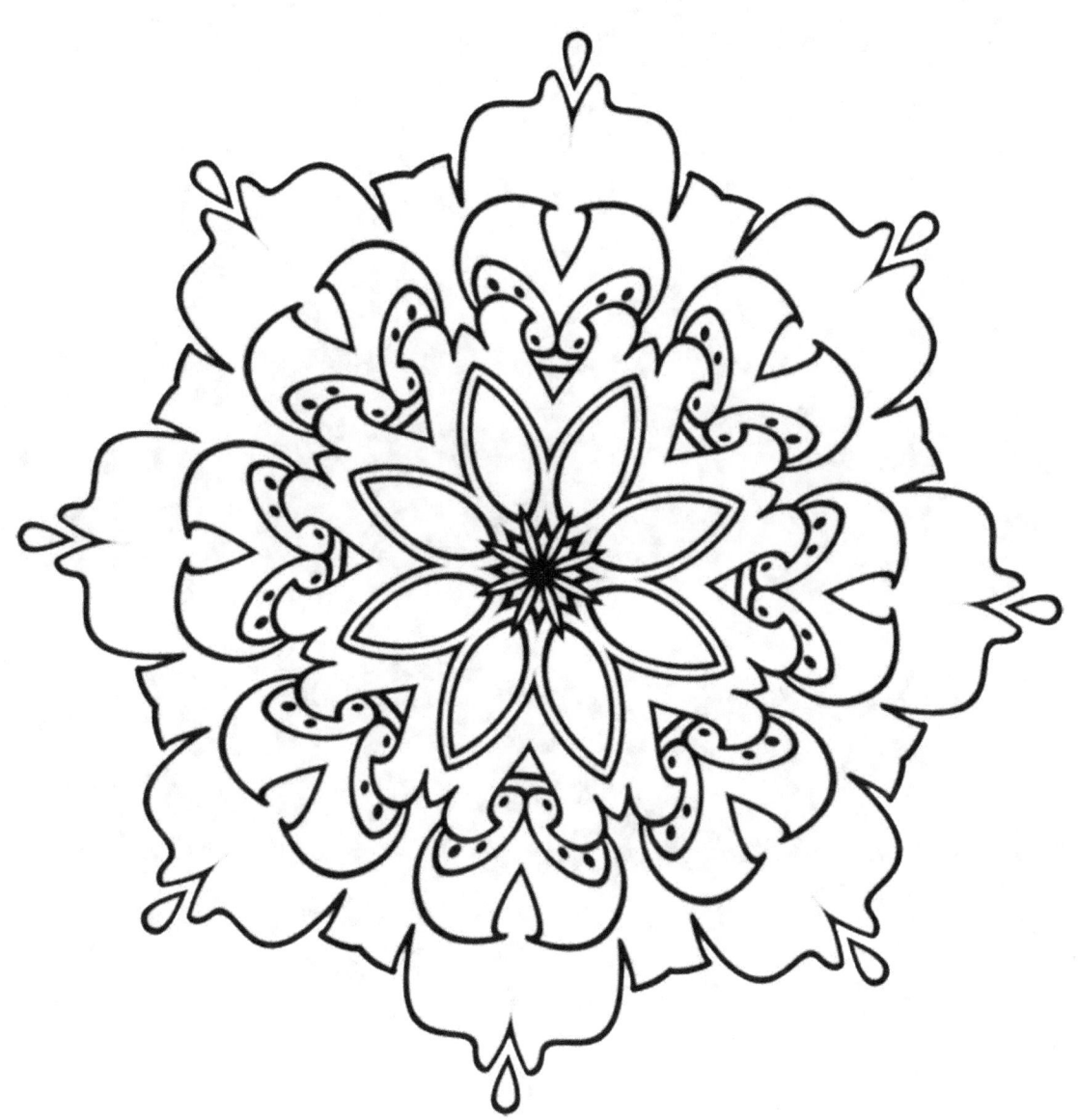

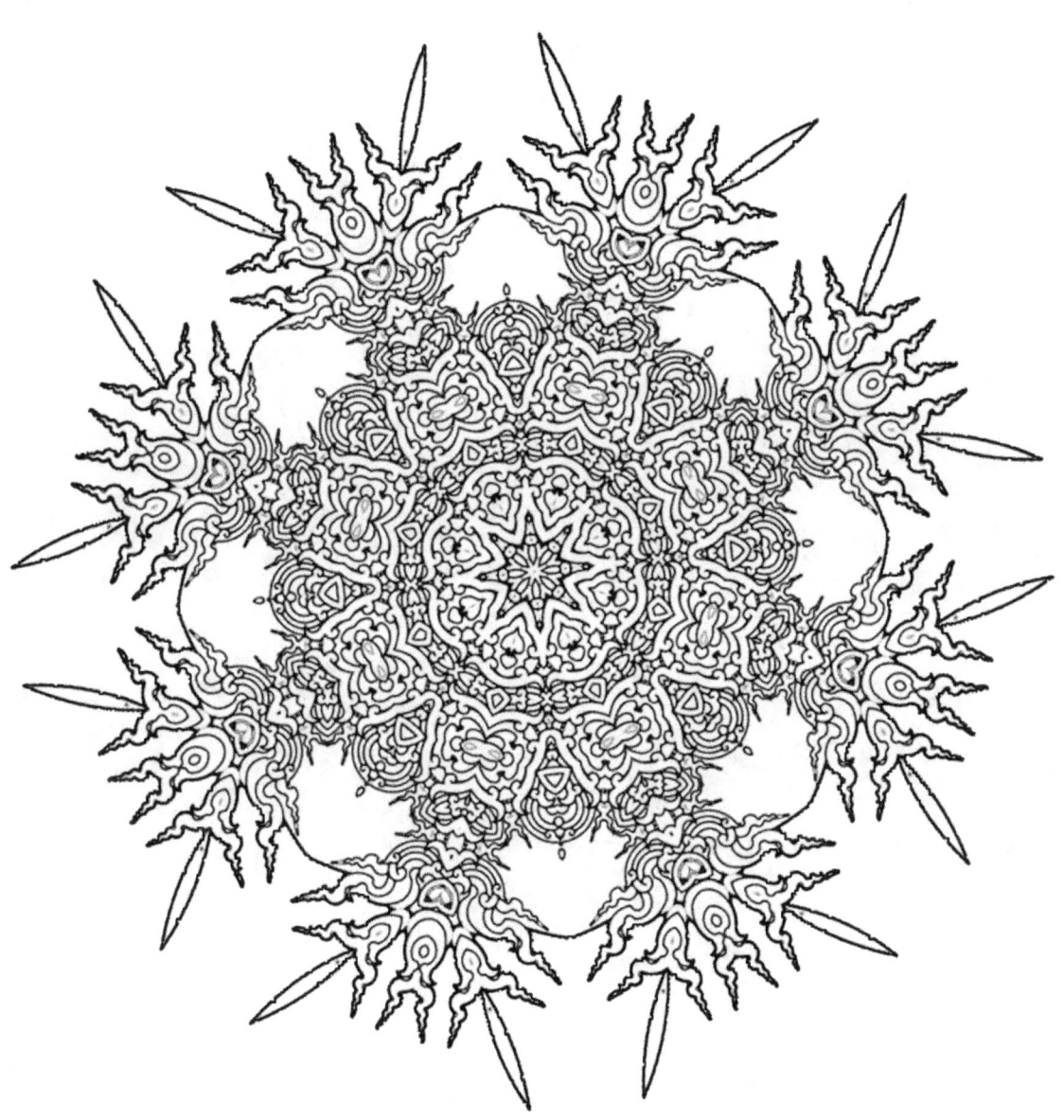

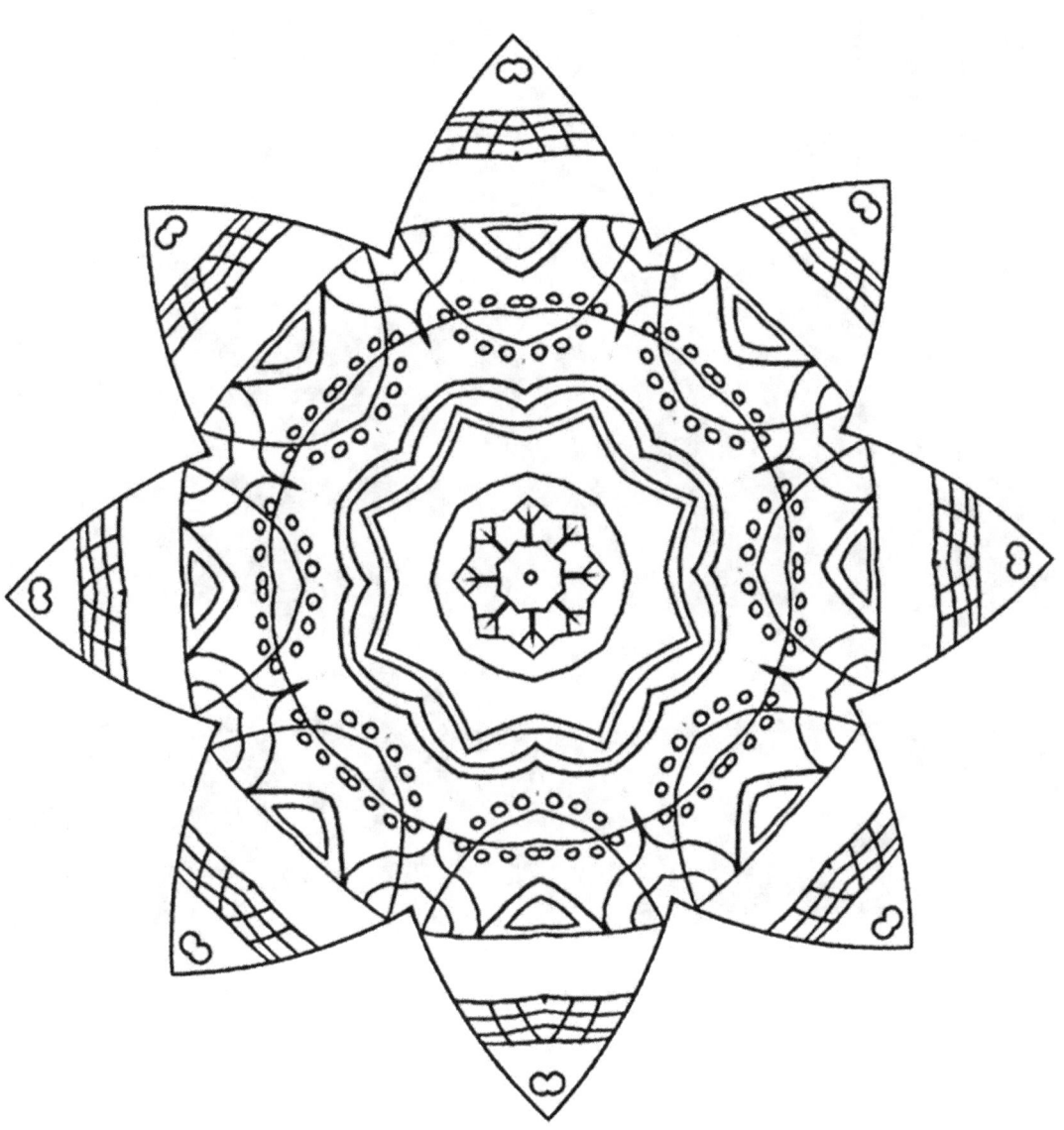

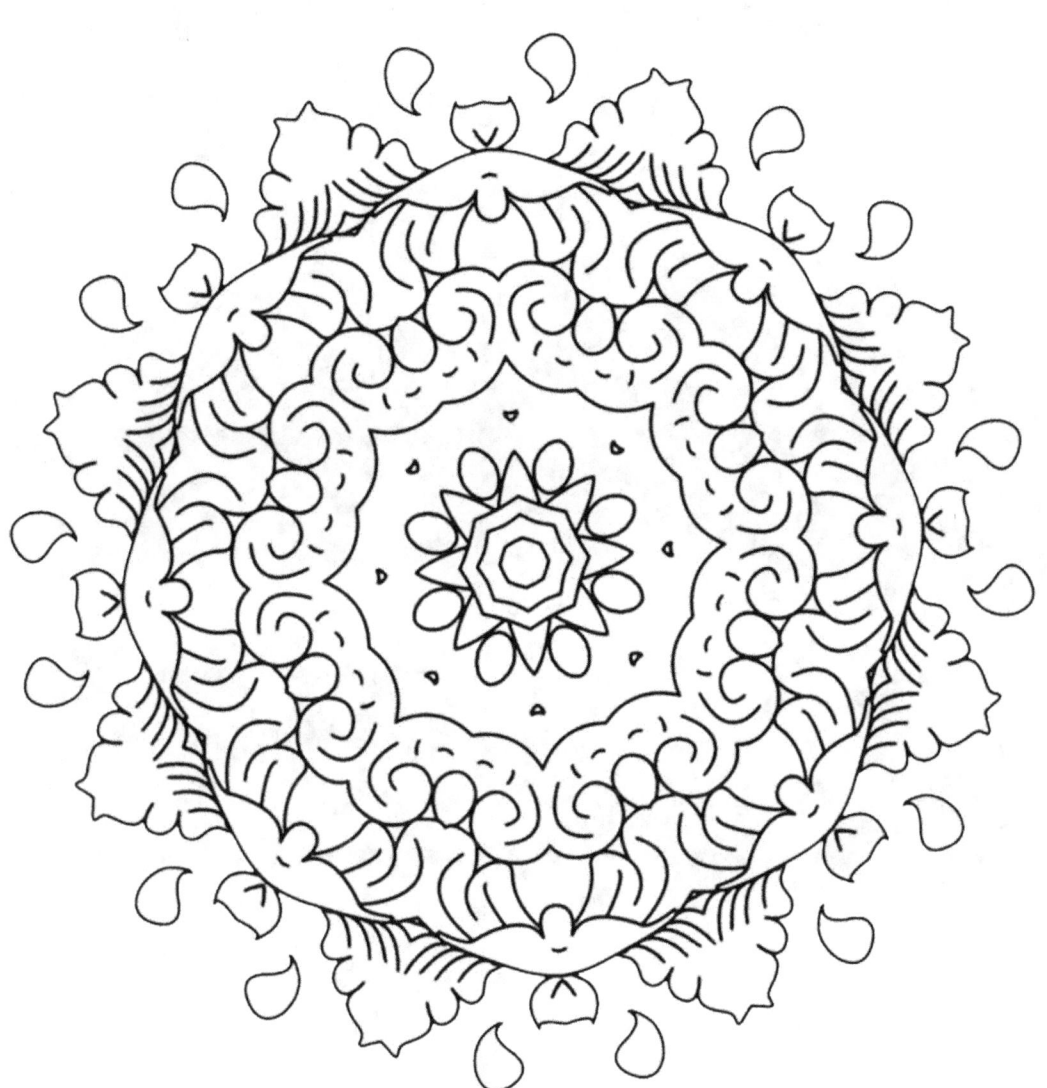

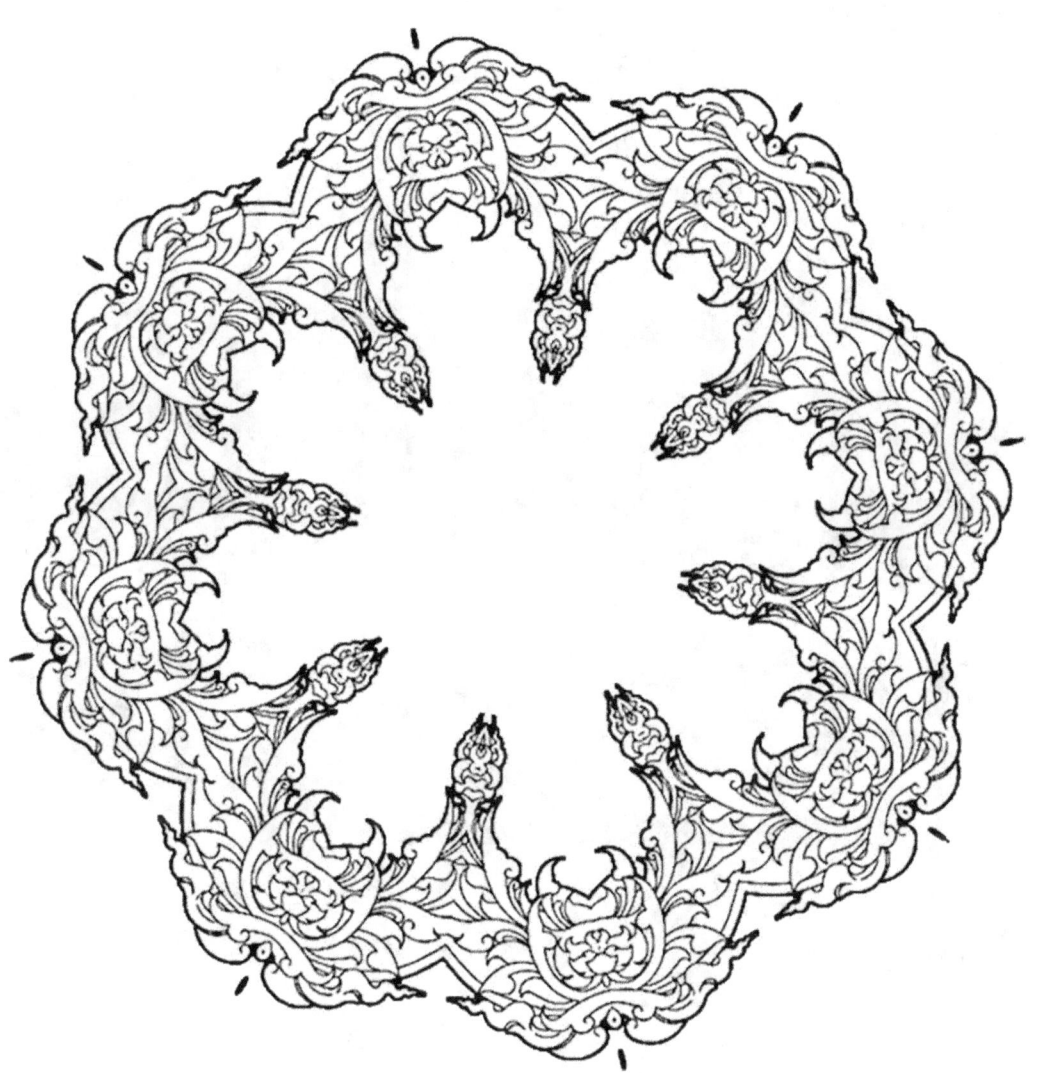

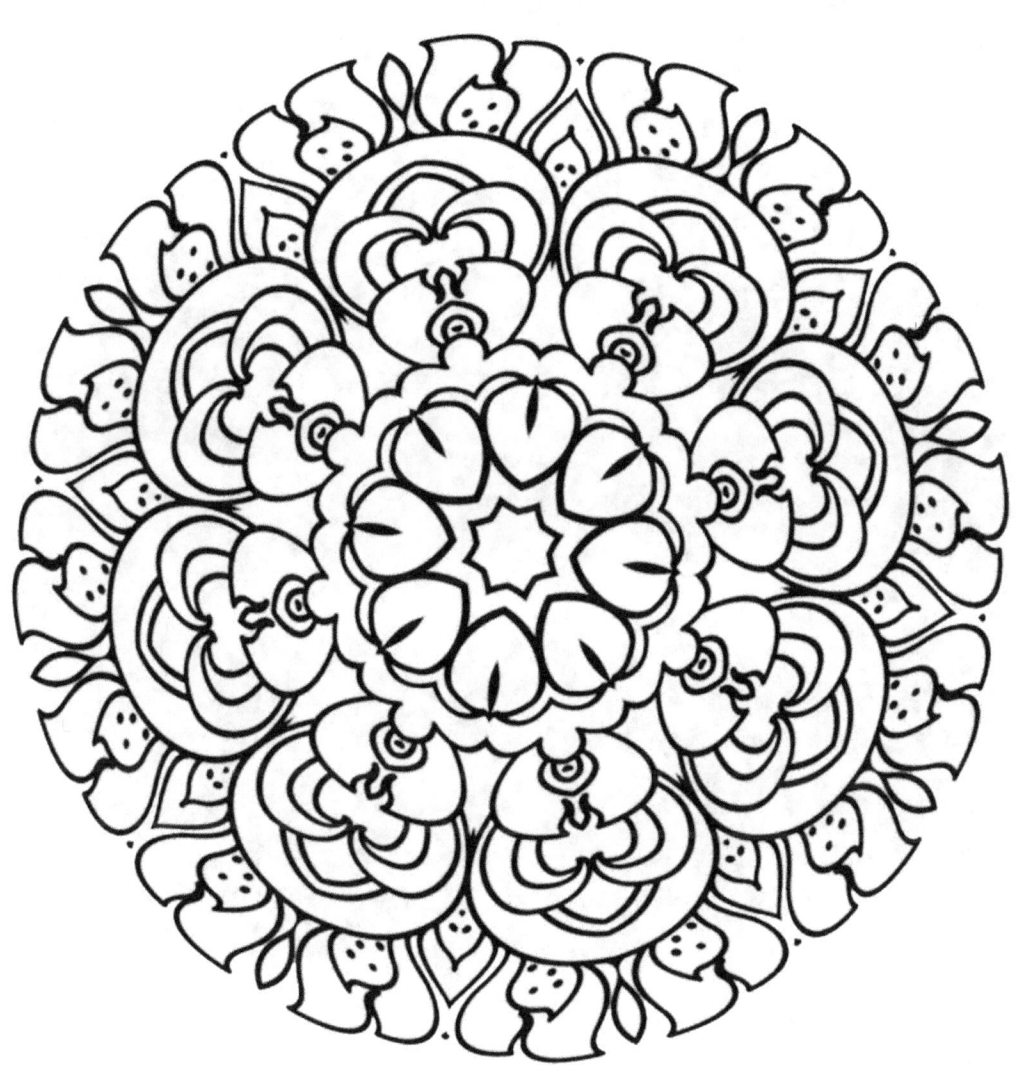

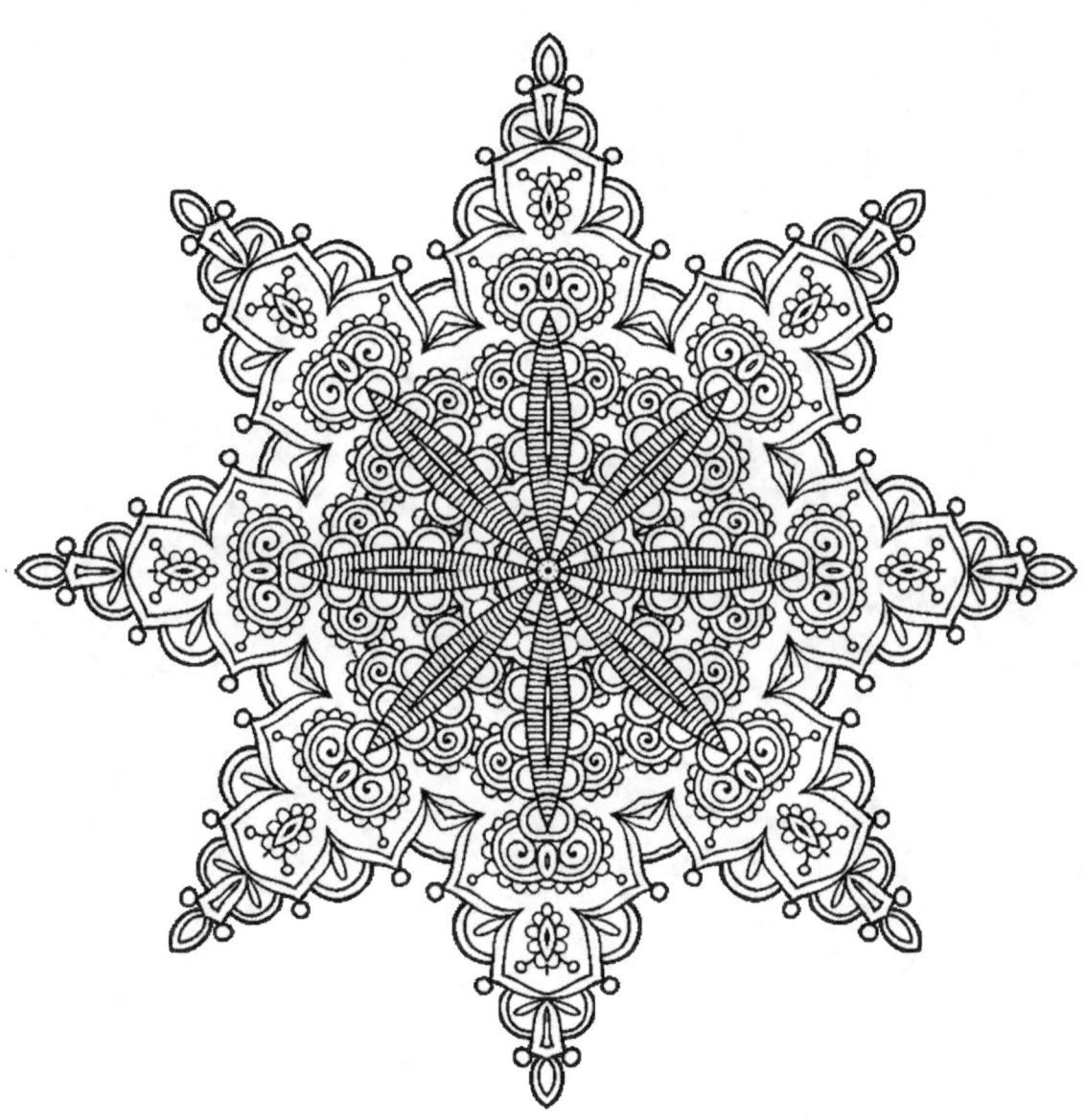

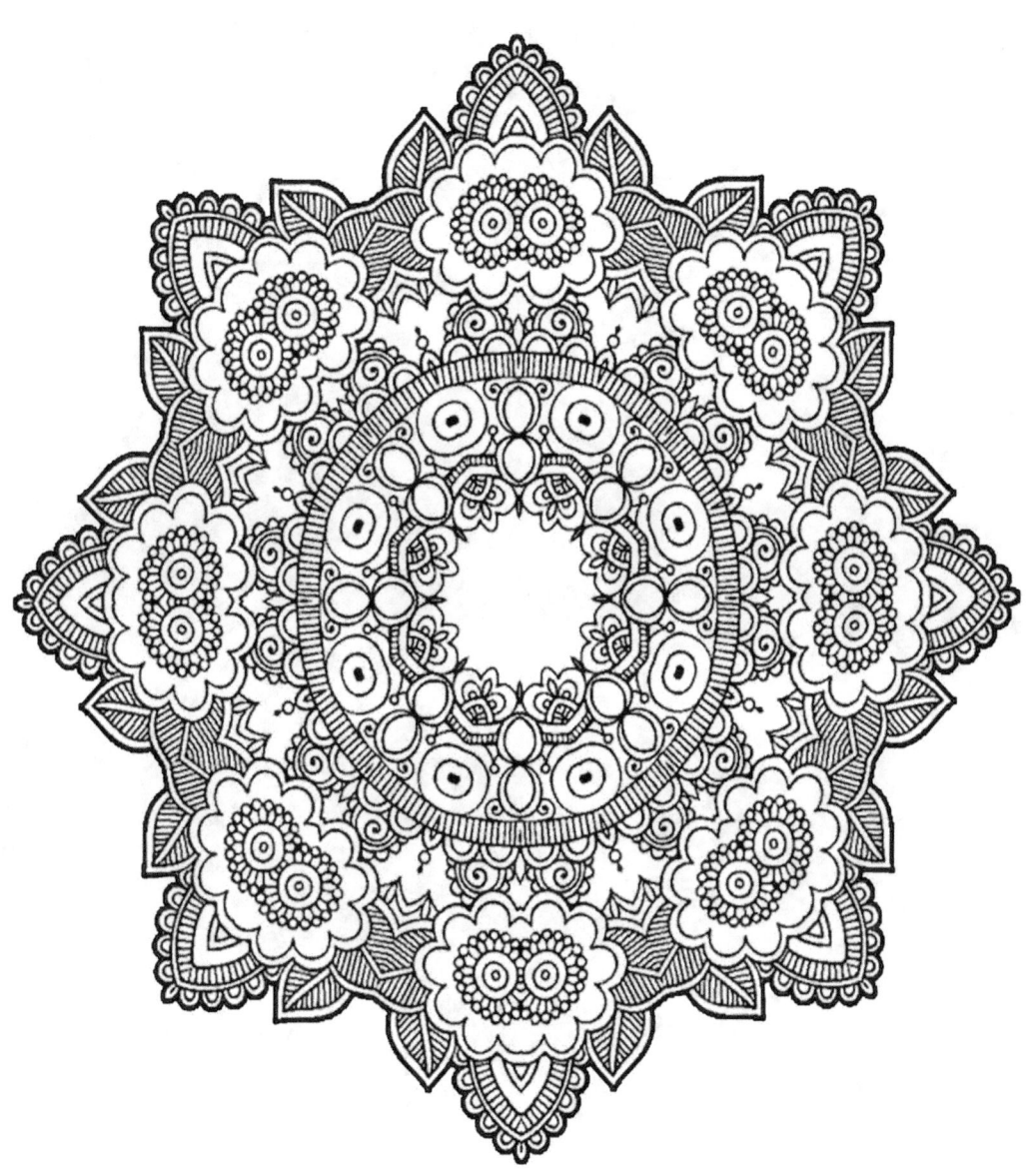

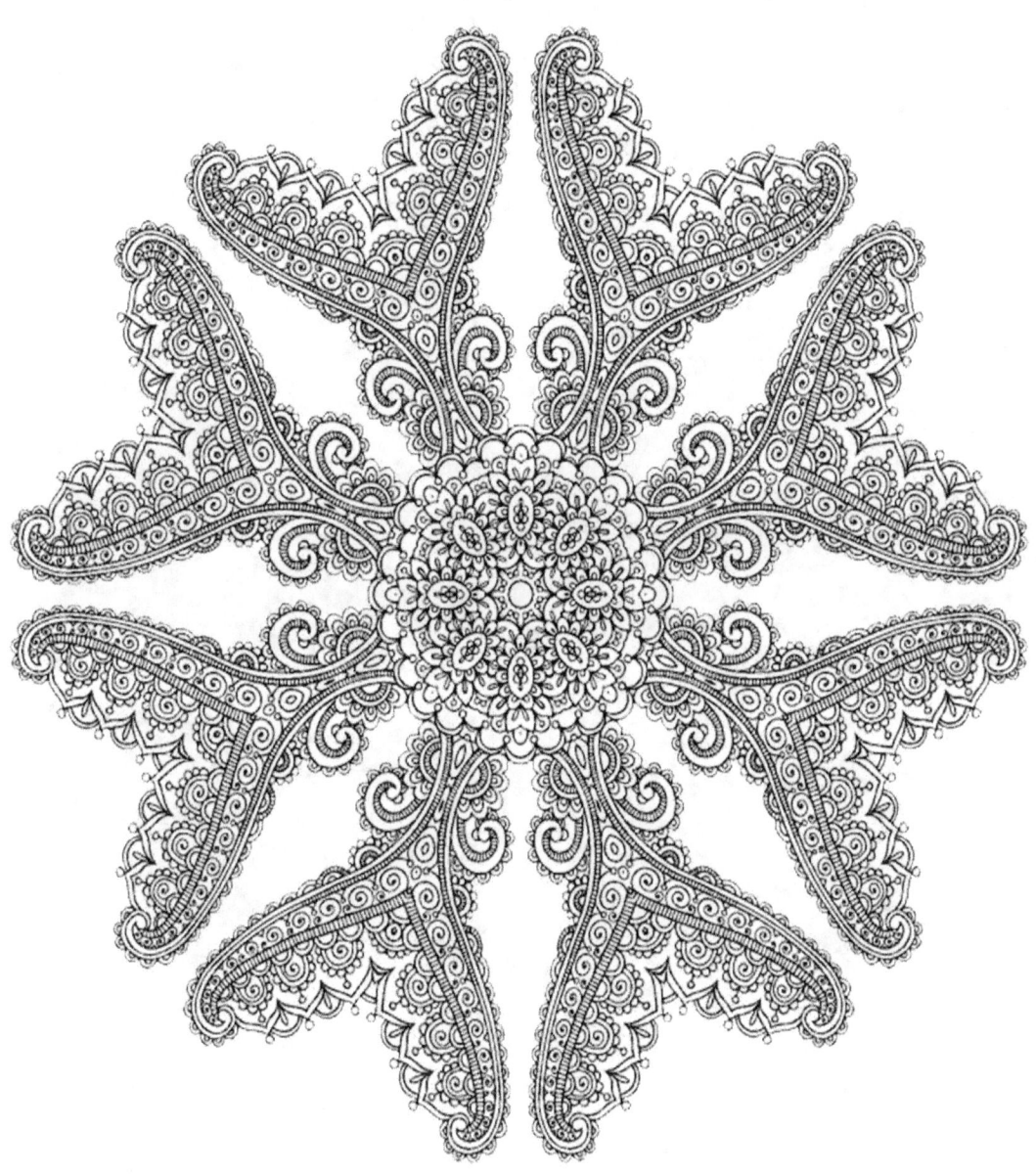